GRATITUDE: THE ULTIMATE TREASURE

SANYAM JAIN

Copyright © Sanyam Jain
All Rights Reserved.

Contents

Foreword

By the immense blessing of almighty god

It's a very proud moment for me to get this book published and more than that, you are about to read this book.

> "*I got the spark for writing books from a natural literary legacy I got from my grandfather, Late. Shri Rawalmal Jain "Mani", author of 108 books, and my father, Shri Sandeep Jain "Mitra", a poet & author.*"

I gained mighty courage to pen down on a topic like Gratitude. This is something, for which, one must be responsible to write. The flame to write my 3rd book ignited just after the launch of my 2nd book, Passion Makes Life Perfect. I was feeling thankful to my destiny and legacy to bless me with my pen. When I was experiencing that thankfulness, I was getting attracted to the word, Gratitude. At that time, I realized, that one can make his day by simply being grateful for his life. I started my research on this topic. I remember, for 74 days, I attended various online sessions on Gratitude and I experienced a mighty change of perspective towards life. Each session demanded a different version of Sanyam Jain and I didn't disappoint myself. Many times I felt like, leave it, live normal, but that creative side of mine never let me settle for less. I continued writing and explored a new version of myself. During my journey of writing days, I realisedrealizedou are grateful, you look into situations from a different perspective, your perception changes, your vision gets clear, you set high standards for your life, and you creaand te an aura of positivity and charm around you, you build a sense of control and understanding in your mind and most importantly, you live more happily.

While I was writing the initial pages of the book, I thought, I need a diverse mindset, different perspectives, and a dedicated soul for this big topic. I asked many people in my social network to come in alliance with me as a co-author of the book. I gained many leads but got one person to sum up as a co-author in this book, Veneesha Jaitwar, we were acquainted with each other, but there was no dedicated connection as such. We talked, we discussed, we agreed and we started writing Gratitude: The Ultimate Treasure.

In the midway, I got a sudden connection with my destiny, I was getting a signal to have goodwill attached in the book, a dedicated guest column where you will get to know the life experience of someone who has already achieved milestones in his/her life. I browsed many familiar faces, pitched many, and discussed with many, but I got the intuition to go with Mrs. Shilpa Agarwal, a model, a businesswoman, and a passion-driven person. I interacted with her and she replied positively. We had a telephonic interaction and were amazed to know about her life journey and how being thankful and positive helped her to reach pinnacles in her life.

This was a small yet beautiful journey to pen down this book, after 8 months of brainstorming, we created a beautiful output and we are glad that this output is currently in your hand.

With all my experience, and understanding, I tried my best to present before you, Gratitude The Ultimate Treasure

Regards

Sanyam Jain

Filmmaker, Entrepreneur, Graphic Designer

CHAPTER I

How I Adapted Gratitude

In the last two chapters, we figured about the concept of gratitude and the power of gratitude and passion. It's good to read such motivation, terminology, and content but it may go in vain if we don't apply it in our daily life. You might be interrogating yourself that the author is saying all about the theory, facts, methods, etc. But is the author himself practicing it? Is the author himself living his so-called life which he states that he is grateful for? 90 percent of you readers are now thinking this. So let me take you on a journey from where I started and how I adapted to a life of gratitude.

I was born in a Jain-Marwari family. A community where 90% of the people either do business or become traditional doctors, engineers, lawyers, or chartered accountants. The other 5% either do the job or go into the stock market. The other 4% go for cracking UPSC. And the remaining 1% are the ones who are apart from all this league.

My mother, grandmother, and their family (before marriage) are typical business-oriented people. But the male species is a bit different. My grandfather was an iconic writer, My father is a poet and the budding me is currently a divine combination of filmmaker, writer, and graphic designer.

But when I connect myself with destiny, the history of my indulgence in this artistic field is a bit mysterious.

There was a period in 2018 when destiny completely turned the small, innocent, kiddish Sanyam Jain into a growned, dynamic, calm but aggressive Sanyam Jain. That was the time when I lost my grandparents, destiny made my father accused before the law and the remains in my family were only me, my mother, and a big house loan bucket that was to be paid off. That was a time when I was completely helpless frustrated and clueless the only support which I got was from my bhua's family. The first 2 months of 2018 were the ultimate test of mine that destiny was taking. In March in March 2018, I gained the courage to take a professional course in animation but it was not so easy to enroll as the fees were around 1 lakh my family somehow made me roll that course because the incident shattered me very bad I started my animation course I learned a lot of things after the completion of my first module when I learn the basics of video editing I was very much curious that how the concept behind any particular video generates. Again destiny changed my path I started researching about that and got to know a new and very glamorous word film making when I was exploring filmmaking I found that my potential and my mind are ready to become a film director. I researched a lot about filmmaking. I started making short films and music videos to practice the process. There was a time when my family said me not to go into this field, but destiny answered all of them again on my behalf, I can't pen the incident but that was completely a game-changing incident. Universe again tested me, I was focused on my journey to learn filmmaking, but now my school threatened me that I won't be allowed to give class 12th board exams. At that time I was a bit scared but being a backbencher in my school life, it didn't bother me much, I ignored them and focused on my Filmmaking, now, the exam time came, and here destiny gave me another tough answer to the universe's exam, that year was 2021, the entire world was facing waves of covid 19. My class 12th board exams got canceled and there was no more happy person than me. It gave me another hint that my destiny and the universe have now mutually decided to see me as a film director. I joined a professional filmmaking institute for my undergraduate program. Here, I expanded my network with various professionals, finely nourished my skills, dedicated all my devotion to my teachers, and never complained about anything, instead adjusted myself accordingly as till this period, I developed a mentality that everything happens for a reason, we may not identify the benefits today, but can do it in future. Among 21 people in my batch, Only two of us got the opportunity to attend a film festival. This gave me another sign that I am going right and receiving the abundance. Our activities stream out of our inside attitude. Frequently, we can hoodwink ourselves by accepting that our interior considerations are private and obscure to people around us. Be that as it may, how we contemplate things and how we process inside will continuously impact how we act ostensibly. While pondering the interior side of being appreciative, includes understanding how we are leaned to process and contemplate things.

*"I am happy because I'm grateful. I choose to be grateful.
That gratitude allows me to be happy"*

-Will Arnett

CHAPTER II

Understanding Gratitude

People perceive gratitude as a very difficult concept.

What do you understand by GRATITUDE?

How about we start with a gratitude definition. You're likely acquainted with communicating appreciation by saying 'thank you when somebody accomplishes something decent for you. However, it's a more extensive idea than just communicating obliged.

Gratitude is characterized as a positive close-to-home response that fills a natural need. It's the enthusiasm for the significant things in our lives.

"It's an assertion of goodness."

We perceive that the wellsprings of this decency are beyond ourselves. We recognize that others or significantly higher powers, assuming you're of a profound outlook — gave us many gifts, of all shapes and sizes, to assist us with accomplishing the decency in our lives.

As we'll see, there are various gratitude rehearses out there that can assist you with improving these abilities. Also, the advantages of doing so can be very astounding.

For what reason is gratitude significant?

While we'll get into the particular advantages of being thankful further down, it's worth focusing on the general significance of gratitude. Even though it can appear to some as a tad of a wooly term, there is a group of logical proof that exhibits its viability.

Incalculable research has demonstrated the way that gratitude can bring an assortment of physical, mental, close to home, and social advantages. It assists us with valuing every one of the positive components of our lives and the individuals in them.

Large numbers of us know about sensations of disappointment - we feel that our lives are deficient and ailing in the things we ache for. At such critical times, to contrast yourself with the untainted appearing lives of others and judge yourself to need. The straightforward act of gratitude can assist with reducing these sentiments.

Let me share one incident with you-

One day I was sitting in a tea stall and having my cup of tea. Two people were running the tea stall. One was looking aged around 70 to 72 years and another was of 9 to 10 years. The grandma went somewhere, that kid was alone at the stall. Two customers came and asked for two cups of tea. The girl gave them the tea. One guy asked for a cigarette. The box of the cigarette was above the shelf. She somehow managed to bring that box down to her and asked him to pick as per his choice as she was not knowing about the cigarette. The man gave him 10 rupees and the girl was having a smile on his face and she thanked God by touching the money on her head. Being a filmmaker, I see everything from a different perspective. This whole incident touched my heart as just to earn a 10 rupees, she gave such a harmful substance to her customer and thanked god later for that 10 rupees. I wonder how cruel destiny can be sometimes with us. I have dedicated a chapter regarding the combined influence of destiny and gratitude in this book.

Is gratitude right for everyone?

Before we get into some of the research and facts behind gratitude, it's important to take a moment to discuss whether practicing gratitude is right for everyone. Although there is a lot of evidence that highlights the benefits of this practice, it isn't the answer for everyone.

Studies suggest that we each have a level of 'trait gratitude', which determines how grateful we can feel. Factors such as genetics, culture, and personality impact this level. It's not known exactly whether a person can 'train' themselves to experience more gratitude.

Similarly, the endless pursuit of happiness can be draining, and life can throw up painful moments without warning. Although there are many benefits of practicing gratitude, it may not be suitable for everyone. Do not be discouraged if you don't feel the effects, and be sure to discuss any mental health issues with your doctor or other medical professionals.

Let us look at this beautiful story to make our perception of gratitude more diverse

A farmer established a peach tree in rich soil.

Under the peach tree, there carried on with a major worm, called a nightcrawler. It went through the dirt by digging passages and afterward utilizing those passages to travel. It came up, normally around evening time and in some cases on wet stormy days, to eat the decaying leaves laying on top of the ground. It reused the leaves by eating them and afterward transforming them into castings to treat the dirt. It dove deep into the ground if the weather conditions above were excessively warm or excessively cold.

Presently the peach tree developed quickly. Each Spring, it awakened. It needed to sprout, develop leaves and greater branches, and lastly when it was mature enough, have an organic product by Summer. Else the farmer could slash it down.

Then in the Fall when it got colder, its leaves would change tone and fall onto the ground. It was lethargic the entire Winter.

As the peach tree developed, it figured out the fact that it was so challenging to develop its foundations straightforwardly into the hard soil. It searched for a simpler way. So it started to develop its underlying foundations into the passages the nightcrawler had made. As the tree developed, its underlying foundations likewise developed, and soon the night crawler's passages were stopped closed.

The nightcrawler couldn't come up for food. Along these lines, to remain alive and hold back from starving, it needed to dig more passages. It could have been done without to do this, since, nightcrawlers are somewhat lethargic.

What's more, the peach tree could have done without shedding its leaves each Fall not long before the virus Winter.

In any case, do you have at least some idea what?

They were both aiding one another, and by doing this, they were helping themselves.

The peach tree needed to shed its leaves which the nightcrawler ate and the worm's castings took care of the peach tree.

Furthermore, the worm needed to dig more passages which permitted the peach tree to become greater so that in the Fall there were a lot of good leaves (and perhaps a peach or two that the farmer missed) for the nightcrawler to eat.

"Also, they lived cheerfully ever later."

Here, both the tree and nightcrawler are grateful towards each other as they both helped each other in some the other way, and that's a simple explanation of being grateful. Every living creature on this planet is connected.

And this connection can be useful for mankind by practicing gratitude. One should always feel grateful for what they have, for what they got, for what they got a precious life to live.

• • •

Being grateful doesn't mean you should feel happy throughout your lifetime but when you are not happy you should make yourself remind of the best things you've experienced and you own which make you happy. Nobody, literally nobody in the world has the power to make you feel good, although some people can support you of course that happiness doesn't last long. Find yourself a way to seek happiness in everything you own. Be grateful for those things eventually you'll understand that everything around you can be the reason for your happiness.

We as a whole need a cheerful life. An incredible work, an ideal family, monetary solidness, and an extraordinary public activity! Also, in this endless quest for bliss that is generally similar to a hallucination, how frequently do we save a moment to thank what we now have present?

It might sound silly, but research exhibits that you would be more joyful assuming you developed a "mentality of gratitude." There's proof to recommend that being appreciative, regardless of your conditions, can work on every aspect of your life, and can acquire more things to be thankful for. The universe listens when you express it, and answers by giving you more things to be appreciative for. That is the enchantment of gratitude.

So what precisely is gratitude and how might you develop it in your lives for a satisfied, positive life?

Gratitude implies gratefulness, remembering your good fortune, seeing basic delights, and recognizing all that you get. It implies figuring out how to carry on with your life as though everything was a marvel and staying alert consistently to the amount you've been given. Subsequently, gratitude likewise assists individuals with associating with an option that could be bigger than themselves as people — whether to others, nature, or a higher power.

Advantages Of Gratitude

Gratitude moves your concentration from what your life needs to the overflow that is now present. Furthermore, the social and mental examination has shown the amazing life enhancements that can come from the act of gratitude. Offering gratitude makes individuals more joyful and stronger, it fortifies connections, it works on physical and emotional wellness, and diminishes pressure.

1. Gratitude Gives You Happiness That Lasts

Heaps of things, from a commendation to a sweet treat, can give little explosions of joy. Gratitude is something that prompts significantly more manageable types of satisfaction since it's not in light of quick delight; it's an outlook. Assuming you consistently set aside some margin to offer thanks and gratefulness, you're probably going to get results. Chasing joy and life fulfillment, gratitude offers an enduring impact in a positive-criticism circle of sorts. Hence, the more gratitude we experience and express, the more circumstances and individuals we might find to offer thanks towards.

2. Works on Mental Health

Individuals who feel thankful experience a decrease in the degree of cortisol, the pressuring chemical. It additionally brings about better heart working and more flexibility to profound difficulties and negative encounters. By rehearsing gratitude we can deal with pressure better compared to other people. By simply recognizing and valuing the easily overlooked details throughout everyday life, we can rework the cerebrum to manage the current conditions with additional mindfulness and more extensive discernment. Showing gratitude can likewise help in:

A) Expressing gratitude can work on your state of mind. Individuals who routinely offer thanks for the positive things in their day-to-day existence are demonstrated to be more joyful generally, prompting lower paces of pressure and sorrow.

B) Showing gratitude can make you more hopeful.
The individuals who offer thanks routinely seem to have a more inspirational perspective on life. Gratitude makes the mind produce an expansion in dopamine (a synapse that is connected with sensations of joy and prize propelled conduct) and serotonin (a synapse accepted to assist with directing temperament and social way of behaving)

C) Helps quiet the psyche
Gratitude assists with quieting the close-to-home cerebrum since it empowers you to break down and answer instead of yielding to your underlying response to what is emerging.

D) Sharing gratitude can assist with decreasing uneasiness and misery
By lessening the pressure chemicals and dealing with the autonomic sensory system capacities, gratitude fundamentally diminishes the side effects of sadness and nervousness. Sensations of gratitude are related to an expansion in the brain tweak of the prefrontal cortex, the mind site answerable for overseeing pessimistic feelings like responsibility, disgrace, and savagery.

3. Actual Health Benefits

Various examinations have inspected the connection between gratitude and actual well-being, like cardiovascular well-being, stress and aggravation, torment discernment, and rest. One investigation discovered that keeping a gratitude diary further developed pulse. Another investigation discovered that zeroing in on things to be appreciative about before bed every night helped with a quiet brain and better rest. One more investigation discovered that individuals who saved a gratitude diary for 15 days revealed fewer migraines, more clear skin, less stomach torment, and diminished clog.

4. Gratitude Facilitates Social Well-Being

Thankful People Have Better connections. Having the option to perceive the decency that another person brings to your life will assist you with valuing that individual more. Gratitude intercessions, for example, considering positive everyday occasions or keeping a gratitude diary can work with social prosperity. Keeping a gratitude journal expanded understudies' feeling of having a place. An investigation discovered that statements of gratitude by administrators persuaded their representatives to be more useful in their everyday work. Gratitude improves sympathy, and thusly, lessens hostility. This is primarily because compassion is the capacity to be delicate toward and figure out individuals' goals and feelings. At the point when people are sympathetic, they are less inclined to be angry and forceful.

5. Works with Better Sleep

With regards to sleep time customs for better rest, gratitude is less notable however presumably undeniably more compelling than cushioning pads or tasting a pleasant cup of green tea. Simply writing down a couple of motivations to feel appreciative before bed could net you an additional half-hour of value rest time.

6. Vocation And Life Goals

One way gratitude can assist you with promoting your objectives is by moving your viewpoint to acknowledge how far you've proactively come. Zeroing in a lot on the parts of your life needing improvement can raise questions about your triumphs. Give yourself credit for handling and overcoming all snags en route. When you genuinely see those things, see how your inspiration to proceed with increments.

To conclude this chapter, When you become arranged toward searching for things to be thankful for, you will find that you start to see the value in basic delights and things that you recently underestimated. Gratitude ought not to be the only response to getting what you need, but an all-the-time gratitude, the sort where you notice the seemingly insignificant details and where you continually search for the great even in terrible circumstances. Today, begin carrying gratitude to your encounters, rather than hanging tight for a good involvement with a request to feel appreciative; along these lines, you'll be on your way toward turning into an expert of gratitude.

Now, you have to understand what is gratitude, now it's the foremost duty of me and my co-author to tell you the universal power of gratitude and passion. See you next chapter.

"Always have an attitude of gratitude"

-Sterling K Brown

CHAPTER III

Power Of Gratitude & Passion

Have you ever thought about how amazing your life would be if you live your passion every day? It seems like just last week when you were that kid who was going to be an astronaut, pilot, or inventor. It probably seems like yesterday when you finished school, got your first job, and charted out your career advancement.

Then something unexpected happened... you grew up.

One region I've moved myself to chip away at is the act of gratefulness. Being grateful falls into place without any issues for some, while others need to buckle down against propensities and tendencies to be an appreciative individuals. I think taking a gander at life from the perspective of gratefulness won't just make you more charming to associate with, it will likewise furnish you with more regular pleasure. Gratefulness is a propensity to be learned - so whether appreciation comes simple to you, I expect that this will assist you with thoroughly considering how to be somebody who is set apart by gratefulness.

At the point when I consider gratefulness, I ordinarily think about it in two classifications: Internal and External.

Again, Our activities stream out of our inside attitude. Frequently, we can hoodwink ourselves by accepting that our interior considerations are private and obscure to people around us. Be that as it may, how we contemplate things and how we process inside will continuously impact how we act ostensibly. While pondering the interior side of being appreciative, includes understanding how we are leaned to process and contemplate things.

Being a grateful individual makes you a more pleasant individual to be near. You're bound to search for the positive and redeemable characteristics in things, which makes an agreeable climate for yourself as well as other people.

Being a grateful individual makes you more useful. Gratefulness breeds energy. Consequently, you're less inclined to flounder in antagonism.

Being a grateful individual makes you more compelling to other people. The more you see the great and the things you must be appreciative of, it becomes irresistible and appealing. It rouses you to need to be appreciative as a result of the life and energy it produces.

HOW I KNOW WHEN I'M AN INTERNALLY THANKFUL PERSON

Whenever I'm inside grateful, I will more often than not center around what I have, not what I'm inadequate with regards to (Glass half full versus half unfilled). I'm ready to see everything to be appreciative for.

Whenever I'm inside grateful, I'm less inclined to whine.

At the point when I'm inside appreciative, it brings about being set apart by happiness. This doesn't mean I quit making and tightening objectives. It implies that I find delight in the things that I now have.

Outside

Outer types of gratefulness are the outward ways we show appreciation for the things that we have and for individuals in our lives. The more that we show appreciation remotely, the more we ponder everything that others have accomplished for us, and the more grateful we become.

The following are two viable ways of starting appearance appreciation remotely:

Verbally

This one is truly clear, to you set it forth plainly: "Say thank you." I'm regularly astounded by the number of chances we that have consistently to tell somebody thank. Try not to fear conveying all you are grateful for in somebody.

Being appreciative verbally doesn't need to be something separate from your typical conversational propensities. Offer and discuss how grateful you are for things. Permit the things you're grateful for to be woven into every discussion you have. Whenever somebody forfeits their time, energy, or assets it's a chance for you to practice verbal gratefulness.

Cards to say thanks

Setting aside some margin to plunk down and work out your gratefulness for somebody is an incredible propensity to shape. In addition to the fact that it is thought to communicate appreciation to somebody, it likewise develops your adoration and warmth for that individual as you consider them. While I'm staying there, I can't help and consider every one of the manners in which I am grateful for that individual in my life.

There are various ways that you can send somebody a note of much appreciation (card, email, message, and so forth.). Here and there sending a message is an incredible method for telling somebody much obliged. Notwithstanding, don't underrate sending somebody a transcribed note. Setting aside some margin to get a card, choosing a pleasant pen, and recording your considerations to impart love and appreciation in a manner that is more private.

I have seasons when I'm better about composing cards to say thanks than others. Generally, this is because I overcomplicate the cycle. It's a nonstop flight. I want to recollect that composing a straightforward "much obliged" is superior to not expressing anything by any stretch of the imagination.

One more fun approach to making your thank you considerably more private is by planning your notes to say thanks. This permits you to tweak the card, make it individual, and straightforwardly relate it to the individual you are sending it to. Once in a while, finding the right card for the right situation is hard. So as of late, I've set aside some margin to assemble a few hand-tailored cards with a portion of my number one individual expressions.

You can plan a card that essentially says thank you or you can get innovative and incorporate words, expressions, or drawings that are well defined for the circumstance.

In some cases, it's difficult to be appreciative. Life can be hard and conditions have an approach to blinding you to every one of the great things in your day-to-day existence you must be appreciative for. Assuming you battle with developing inner thanksgiving, a decent spot to begin is with outer articulations. After some time, you'll make propensities for appreciation - which will impact both your inside and outer articulations of gratefulness.

You might be posing the inquiry: "Where do I start if I need to be a grateful individual? Do I start with the inward and assess my considerations and demeanor or do I set in motion ways of behaving that express appreciation?" The response to this question is yes - you ought to do both. It's great to assess yourself and comprehend the reason why you do the things you do and how that impacts your demeanor of being appreciative. It's similarly essential to incorporate ways of behaving that express gratefulness as well as work up thanksgiving in your heart.

What does it mean to grow up anyway?

While society wants you to believe living your passion is irresponsible and foolish, we are going to focus on 10 amazing things that happen when you live your passion and feel grateful for everything that happened to you-

1. Expanded Self-Confidence

There is a secret truth that everybody needs to be acknowledged for what their identity is. However, everybody isn't open to communicating what their identity is. At the point when you overlook the assessments of others and live your PASSION, you will turn out to be more open to communicating.

As a rule, when you are not experiencing your energy, you are carrying on with the existence that you accept is worthy to other people. Your certainty will endure when you surrender to the pressing factors of society, your companions, and your family. This is to a great extent since you are compelling yourself to accomplish something that is of little interest to you.

2. Lower Stress Levels

The individuals who live their passion have an inner inspiration that carries equilibrium to their circumstances. Thus, they will doubtlessly have upsetting circumstances that go back and forth. A genuine model would be you, who have three significant undertakings that should be finished around the same time. Consequently, you feel focused until the day is finished.

The individuals who are not experiencing their passion are generally detesting their work and think that it's upsetting each day. The demonstration of awakening, getting into their garments, and crashing into work stresses them. They fear each Monday and long for each Friday.

3. Satisfaction in Your Work

As we began to address, there isn't anything more depleting than "working to live." You feel stuck because you have bills to pay and your work covers the tabs.

Even though there is a touch of vulnerability encompassing your energy, you can't think little of the benefit of cherishing what you do.

By seeking your passion, you will feel satisfied with your work. You will have the delight of living your energy, rather than intending to live your passion. There isn't anything more compensating than doing what you were called to do.

4. Authority of Work-Life Balance

There is an idiom that if you live your passion, you at this point don't require a work-life balance. The reason is work-life balance is possibly required when your work is depleting.

At the point when you are following your energy, your life is inconsistent in equilibrium. Your work doesn't feel like work since you would do it for nothing.

Would you be able to envision, wishing you could be working since you appreciate what you do? All things considered, that is actually what will happen when you are seeking after your passion.

5. Less Regrets Later in Life

Envision what your life would resemble on the off chance that you sought after everything you could ever want and interests. Presently suppose you ran into that individual and needed to disclose to him why you didn't seek after your passion. This is the genuine discussion a great many people are having when it is everything except past the point of no return.

Face a challenge and wager on yourself. Regardless of whether it doesn't work out precisely as you would have trusted, you will be better for it.

6. Self-improvement

The explanation a great many people don't live their passion as a result of the vulnerability encompassing their energy. You may have questions concerning your capacity to succeed financially, expertly, or even inwardly.

Now and then, you are on the whole correct to think thusly. This doesn't mean you ought to acknowledge this reality and fail to address it. All things being equal, invest some energy building up the range of abilities expected to achieve your passion.

You can turn into a scientific genius on the off chance that you need to be a space traveler. You can practice and seek after your pilot's permit on the off chance that you need need to be a pilot.

7. Positive Attraction

Some of the time you dread that your energy won't be gotten well by others. The thing about carrying on with a not exactly legitimate life is you will draw in some unacceptable individuals.

At the point when you carry on with your life and follow your interests, you will pull in similarly invested individuals.

Truth be told, you are likely going to annoy a few people when you are seeking after your energy. Individuals don't care for change and when you change, it could change your connections.

Try not to leave this alone something that will keep you down, however. Your development is attached to your readiness to seek after the convictions that will empower you to accomplish your objective.

8. Grow Your Comfort Zone

Try not to fall into the snare of accepting that you need to surrender everything to follow your passion. These sorts of restricting convictions keep the vast majority from truly beginning their excursion to transform them.

Truth be told, you don't have to quit any pretense of everything to begin once more. Here's the reason.

Permit yourself to gradually extend your usual range of familiarity and attempt new things. You can keep on carrying on with your current life while seeking new undertakings as an afterthought.

As you develop more agreeable in your capacity to live your passion, you can gradually move additional time towards it. Before you know it, you will be in with no reservations and make every moment count.

9. Be Grateful

The facts confirm that you can and ought to be appreciative constantly. There is continually something to be thankful for in your life. Regardless of whether you got a punctured tire on your path home from work, at any rate, you have a vehicle.

Also, you ought to consistently be appreciative to have work. However, there is little uncertainty that you will feel more thankful if you are accomplishing something you are energetic consistently. You could sensibly wind up eager to get up each day since you realize it is one more day to satisfy your life's motivation.

At the point when you seek after your passion, you are fulfilled and content with the world, and you will be kinder to other people.

10. Release Your Creativity

The thing about carrying on with a daily existence missing your passion is that you are no doubt living the normally strolled way. Security in life is frequently the nonattendance of inventiveness.

At the point when you leave the easy way out and begin to live your passion, you should release your imagination to succeed. You will be wandering into unknown waters in your day-to-day existence and it tends to be threatening. However, that is the place where the enchantment occurs.

At the point when you get yourself eye to eye with an obstruction logged among you and your passion, you need to trust in yourself that you will win.

The word 'powerful' is itself a very small entity to define gratefulness to be so great. A person can only understand the meaning and positive impacts of gratefulness by practicing it. Gratitude has its mighty powers, it gives people joy, and hence it helps them to get rid of stress.

Now, when you're grateful for everything around you and about everything you own, you find a way for yourself to be happy in every situation no matter how bad it is. When you develop such qualities to get comfortable with your problems, they seem very small compares to the things that can make you happy.

When a person is happy dopamine and Serotonin are released in the brain which helps with motivation and also regulates sleep which helps the brain to work with its full potential which in turn makes a person a better problem solver and also a good decision maker i.e. your mental health is good and you are a mentally a strong person now, who can strongly react to bad situations in the life. Nowadays being a person relieved from stress make you outshine the crowd because many people in today's world worry about small things which eventually makes them stressed. Outshining the crowd can also make you more confident.

Summing up being grateful makes you more confident, happy, and relieved to deal with problems.

"We learned about gratitude and humility - that so many people had a hand in our success"

Michelle Obama

CHAPTER IV

You Are Destined

There is, and consistently has been far-reaching confidence in Fate, or Destiny, that is to say, in an everlasting and uncertain Power that distributes unmistakable closures to the two people and countries. This conviction has emerged from the long perception of the unavoidable truths that apply to everyone.

Men are cognizant that there are sure events that they have no control over, and are frail to turn away. Birth and passing, for example, are unavoidable, and large numbers of the episodes of life show up similarly inescapable.

Men strain each nerve for the fulfillment of unavoidable finishes, and continuously they become aware of a Power which is by all accounts not of themselves, which disappoints their weak endeavors, and giggles, figuratively speaking, at their vain endeavoring and battle.

As men advance throughout everyday life, they figure out how to submit, pretty much, to this overruling Power which they don't have any idea, seeing just its belongings in themselves and their general surroundings, and they call it by different names, like God, Providence, Fate, Destiny, and so on.

Men of consideration, like artists and savants, move to one side, so to speak, to watch the developments of this secretive Power as it appears to hoist its top choices from one perspective, and strike down its casualties on the other, without reference to the legitimacy or bad mark.

The best writers, particularly the sensational artists, address this Power in their works, as they have noticed it in Nature. The Greek and Roman writers normally portray their legends as having the foresight of their destiny and taking the means to get away from it, yet thusly they aimlessly include themselves in a progression of results that achieve the destruction which they are attempting to deflect. Shakespeare's characters, then again, are addressed, as in Nature, with no prescience (besides as presentiment) of their specific predetermination. Subsequently, as indicated by the writers, regardless of whether the man knows his destiny, he can't deflect it, and each cognizant or oblivious demonstration of his is a stage towards it.

"The Moving Finger composes, and having writ, Moves on: nor all thy Piety nor Wit

Will bait it back to drop a portion of a line, Nor all thy Tears wash out a Word of it."

Subsequently, men in all countries and times have encountered in their lives the activity of this strong Power of Law, and in our country today this experience has been solidified in the curt adage, "Man proposes, God, arranges."

Be that as it may, problematic as it might show up, there is a similarly broad faith in man's liability as a free specialist.

All ethical training is a confirmation of man's opportunity to pick his course and form his fate: and man's patient and untiring endeavors in accomplishing his finishes are statements of awareness of opportunity and power.

This double insight of destiny from one viewpoint, and opportunity from different, has led to the endless debate between the professors in Fatalism and the upholders of through and through freedom — a contention which was as of late resuscitated under the expression "Determinism versus Freewill."

Between obviously clashing limits there is dependably a "center way" of equilibrium, equity, or remuneration which, while it incorporates the two limits, can't be supposed to be either, and which brings both into concordance; and this center way may be the resource between two limits.

Truth can't be sectarian, in any case, by its tendency, is the Reconciler of limits; thus, regarding this situation which we are thinking about, there is a "brilliant actually imply" which brings Fate and Free will into a cozy relationship, wherein, to be sure, it is seen that these two unquestionable realities in human existence, for such they are, are nevertheless two parts of one focal regulation, one bringing together and sweeping rule, in particular, the law of causation in its ethical viewpoint.

Moral causation requires both Fate and Free will, both an individual obligation and individual destiny, for the law of causes should likewise be the law of impacts, and circumstances and logical results should constantly be equivalent; the train of causation, both in issue and psyche, should be endlessly adjusted, along these lines interminably, everlastingly great. Hence every impact might be supposed to be a thing destined, yet the foreordaining power is a reason and not the fiat of an erratic will.

Man ends up engaged with the train of causation. His life is comprised of circumstances and results. It is both planting and harvesting. Each demonstration of his is a reason which should be adjusted by its belongings. He picks the reason (this is Free will), he can't pick, modify, or turn away the impact (this is Fate); subsequently, Free will represent the ability to start causes, and predetermination is a contribution to impacts.

It is thusly a fact that man is foreordained to unavoidable closures, however, he, at the end of the day, has (however he knows it not) given the command; that great or underhanded thing from which there can be no getting away, he has, by his deeds, achieved.

It might here be asked that man isn't answerable for his deeds, that these are the impacts of his personality, and that he isn't liable for the person, positive or negative, which was given to him at his introduction to the world. Assuming a person was "given him" upon entering the world, this would be valid, and there would then be no ethical regulation, and no requirement for moral education; however characters are not given instant, they are developed; they are, to be sure, impacts, the results of the ethical regulation itself, that is — the results of deeds.

Character aftereffect of an amassing of deeds which have been stacked up, as it were, by the person during his life.

Man is the practitioner of his deeds; as such he is the producer of his personality; and as the practitioner of his deeds and the creator of his personality, he is the disintegrate and shaper of his fate. He can adjust and modify his deeds, and each time he acts he alters his personality, and with the change of his personality for good or malevolence, he is foreordaining for himself new predeterminations — fates terrible or valuable as per the idea of his deeds. Character is predetermination itself; as a decent blend of deeds, it bears inside itself the consequences of those deeds. These outcomes lie concealed as moral seeds in obscurity openings of the person, anticipating their time of germination, development, and fruitage.

Those things which come upon a man are simply the reflections; that predetermination which sought after him, which he was frail to escape by exertion, or on the other hand, deflects by supplication, was the tireless demon of his off-base deeds requesting and authorizing compensation; those gifts and reviles which come to him unbidden are the resounding reverberations of the sounds which he sent forward.

It is this information on the Perfect Law dealing with or more all things; of the Perfect Justice working in and changing every single human undertaking, that empowers the great man to cherish his foes, and to transcend all contempt, disdain, and grumbling; for he knows that main his own can come to him, and that, however, he is encircled by persecutors, his foes are nevertheless the visually impaired instruments of impeccable revenge; thus he faults them not, yet serenely accepts his records, and quietly pays his ethical obligations.

However, this isn't all; he doesn't just compensate for his obligations; he takes care not to get any further obligations. He watches himself and makes his deeds flawless. While taking care of detestable records, he is laying up great records. By stopping his wrongdoing, he is finishing underhanded and languishing.

What's more, presently let us consider how the Law works specifically in cases in the manifestation of fate through deeds and character. In the first place, we will see this current life, for the present is the union of the whole past; the net consequence of all that a man has at any point thought and done is held inside him. It is recognizable that occasionally the great man comes up short and the deceitful man thrives — a reality which appears to put all ethical sayings with regards to the great consequences of nobility out of record — and along these lines, many individuals keep the activity from getting any only regulation in human existence, and even pronounce that it is mainly crooked that succeed.

By and by, the ethical regulation exists, and isn't changed or undermined by shallow ends. It ought to be recalled that man is a changing, developing being. The great man was not generally great; the terrible man was not awful all the time. Indeed, even in this life, there was a period, in countless examples, when the one who is currently, was vile; when he who is presently kind, was horrible; when he who is currently unadulterated, was sullied.

On the other hand, there was a period in this life, in various examples, when he who is currently unfair, was simple; when he who is presently brutal, was thoughtful; when he who is presently unclean, was unadulterated. Consequently, the great man who is surpassed with disaster today is procuring the aftereffect of his previous evil planting; later he will harvest the blissful consequence of his current great planting; while the awful man is presently procuring the consequence of his previous great planting; later he will harvest the aftereffect of his present planting of terrible.

Attributes are fixed propensities for the mind, the consequences of deeds. A demonstration rehashed countless times become oblivious or programmed — that is, it then, at that point, appears to rehash the same thing with practically no work concerning the practitioner, so it appears to him extremely difficult to avoid it, and afterward it has turned into a psychological trademark.

Here is an unfortunate man unemployed. He tells the truth and isn't a shirker. He needs work, and can't get it. He makes a respectable attempt and keeps on coming up short.

Where could the equity in his parcel be? There was a period in this man's condition when he had a lot of work. He felt troubled with it; he evaded it and yearned for ease. He figured how superb it is to sit around aimlessly.

He didn't see the value in the blessedness of his parcel. His craving for ease is presently satisfied, however, the organic product for which he yearned, and which he thought would taste so sweet, has gone to cinders in his mouth. The condition which he went for the gold, sit around aimlessly, he has reached, and there he is constrained to stay till his example is entirely scholarly.

Furthermore, he is discovering that ongoing straightforwardness is corrupting, that to not have anything to do is a state of horror, and that work is a respectable and favored thing. His previous cravings and deeds have brought him where he is; and presently his current longing for work, his endless looking and requesting it, will similarly as unquestionably achieve its useful outcome. Done craving inaction, his current condition will, as an impact, the reason for which is not generally proliferated, before long pass away, and he will get business; and on the off chance that his entire brain is presently set on work, and he wants it regardless of anything else, then, at that point, when it comes he will be overpowered with it; it will stream into him from all sides, and he will succeed in his industry.

Then, at that point, on the off chance that he doesn't comprehend the law of circumstances and logical results in human existence, he will ask why work comes to him unsought, while other people who look for it arduously neglect to get it. Nothing comes unbidden; where the shadow is, there likewise is the substance. That which comes to the individual is the result of his deeds.

As merry industry prompts more noteworthy industry and expanding flourishing, and work evaded or embraced discontentedly prompts a lesser level of work and diminishing success, so with every one of the changed states of life as we see them — they are the predeterminations created by the contemplations and deeds of every specific person. So likewise with the immense assortment of characters — they are the maturing and aged development of the planting of deeds.

As the individual gets what he asks for, the country is a local area of people, harvests likewise what it plants. Countries become extraordinary when their chiefs are simply men; they fall and blur when their equitable men die. The people who are in power set a model, positive or negative, for the whole country.

Extraordinary will be the harmony and thriving of a country when there will emerge inside it a line of legislators who, having first laid down a good foundation for themselves in grand respectability of character, will coordinate the energies of the country toward the way of life of excellence and improvement of character, knowing that main through private industry, trustworthiness, and honorability might public success at any point continuing.

In any case, most importantly, is the Great Law, tranquility and reliable equity dispensing to humans their transitory fates, tear-smudged or grinning, the texture of their hands. Life is an incredible school for the improvement of character, and all, through difficulty and battle, bad habits and ideals, achievement and disappointment, are gradually learning the examples of shrewdness.

THE WOW OF SELF-CONTROL

We live in a logical age. Men of science are numbered by thousands, and they are constantly looking, investigating, and trying different things with a view to revelation and the increment of information.

The racks of our libraries, both public and private, are weighty with their heap of forcing volumes on logical subjects, and the superb accomplishments of present-day science are generally before us — whether in our homes or our roads, in nation or town, ashore or ocean — there will we have before us some radiant gadget, some new achievement of science, for adding to our solace, speeding up, or saving the work of our hands.

However, with all our huge store of logical information, and its frightening and quickly expanding brings about the universe of disclosure and creation, there is, in this age, one part of science that has so far fallen into rot as to have become practically neglected; a science, in any case, which is of more noteworthy significance than the wide range of various sciences joined, and without which all science would yet support the finishes of childishness, and help in man's obliteration — I allude to the Science of Self-control. Our cutting-edge researchers concentrate on the components and powers which are outside themselves, with the object of controlling and using them. The people of yore concentrated on the components and powers which were inside themselves, with the end goal of controlling and using them, and the people of yore delivered such strong Masters of information toward this path, that right up to the present day they are held in adoration as divine beings, and the tremendous strict associations of the world depend on their accomplishments.

Magnificent similar to the powers in nature, they are immeasurably substandard compared to that mix of wise powers which contain the psyche of man, and which rule and direct the visually impaired mechanical powers of nature.

Accordingly, that's what it follows, to grasp, control, and direct the inward powers of enthusiasm, want, will, and acumen is to be in control of the fates of men and countries.

As in customary science, there are, in this heavenly science, levels of fulfillment; and a man is perfect in information, extraordinary in himself, and incredible in his effect on the world, in the action that he is perfect indiscretion.

He who gets it and rules the powers of outside nature is the normal researcher, yet he who gets it and overwhelms the inward powers of the psyche is the heavenly researcher; and the regulations which work in acquiring information on outer appearances, work likewise in acquiring information on inner assortments.

A man can't turn into a cultivated researcher in half a month or months, nay, not even in a couple of years. Be that as it may, solely after numerous long stretches of meticulous examination might he at any point talk with power, and be positioned among the bosses of science. In like manner, a man can't gain discretion, and become had of the insight and harmony giving information which that restraint presents, yet by numerous long periods of patient work; a work which is even more challenging because it is quiet, and both unnoticed and neglected by others; and he who might seek after this science effectively should figure out how to remain solitary, and work unrewarded, all things considered.

The normal researcher seeks after, in securing his specific sort of information, the accompanying five organized and consecutive advances:

1. **Observation:** that is, he intently and diligently notices the current realities of nature.

2. **Experiment:** Having become familiar, by rehashed perceptions, with specific realities, he tries different things with those realities, with a view to the revelation of normal regulations. He puts his realities through inflexible cycles of investigation, thus finding out what is futile and what of worth; and he dismisses the previous and holds the last option.

3. **Classification:** Having collected and confirmed a mass of realities by countless perceptions and examinations, he starts to characterize those realities, to orchestrate them in precise gatherings with the object of finding some basic regulation, some covered up and binding together standard, which oversees, manages, and ties together these realities.

4. **Deduction:** Thus he gives the fourth step of derivation. From current realities and results which are before him, he finds specific perpetual methods of activity and subsequently uncovers the secret laws of things.

5.**Knowledge:** Having demonstrated and laid out specific regulations, it could be said to describe such a man that he knows. He is a researcher, a man of information.

Be that as it may, the fulfillment of logical information isn't the end, incredible for all intents and purposes. Men don't achieve information for themselves alone, nor to keep it locked subtly in their souls, similar to a lovely gem in a dull chest. The finish of such information is used, administration, and the increment of the solace and joy of the world. Subsequently, when a man has turned into a researcher, he gives the world the advantage of his insight and unselfishly presents to humankind the consequences of every one of his works.

In this way, in past information, there is a further advance of Use: that is, the right and unselfish utilization of the information procured; the use of information to development for the normal weal.

It will be noticed that the five stages or cycles specified continue the inefficient progression and that no man can turn into anyone researcher of them. Without the initial step of deliberate perception, for example, he was unable to try and enter the domain of information on nature's mysteries.

From the get-go, the searcher for such information has before him a universe

of things: these things he doesn't have any idea; a significant number of them, without a doubt, appear to be hopelessly gone against one to the next, and there is evident disarray; yet by quietly and relentlessly chasing after these five cycles, he finds the request, nature, and characters of things; sees the focal regulation or regulations which tie them together in an amicable relationship, thus stops disarray and obliviousness.

Similarly as with the regular researcher, so with the heavenly researcher; he should seek after, with similar selfless tirelessness, five moderate strides in the achievement of self-information, and poise. These five stages are equivalent to with the normal researcher, yet the cycle is switched, the brain, rather than being focused upon outside things, is turned around upon itself, and the examinations are sought after in the domain of psyche (of one's psyche) rather than in that of issue.

Right away, the searcher for divine information is defied with that mass of wants, interests, feelings, thoughts, and intellections which he calls himself, which is the premise of every one of his activities, and from which his life continues.

This blend of undetectable, yet strong, powers shows up confusedly; some of them stand, evidently, in direct clash with one another, with no appearance or any expectation of compromise; his brain completely, as well, with his life which continues from that psyche, doesn't appear to have any fair connection to numerous different personalities and lives about him, and by and large, there is a state of agony and disarray from which he would fain escape.

In this way, he starts by definitely understanding his condition of obliviousness, for nobody could gain either regular or heavenly information, assuming he was persuaded that without study or work he previously had it. With such an impression of one's obliviousness, there comes the longing for information, and the beginner in poise enters upon the rising pathway, in which are the accompanying five stages:

1. Introspection. This agrees with the perception of the regular researcher. The psychological eye is turned like a searchlight upon the inward things of the brain, and its unpretentious and steadily differing processes are noticed and painstakingly noted. This moving to one side from childish delights, from the energies of common joys and aspirations, to notice, with the object of grasping, one's inclination, is the start of discretion. Until now, the man has been indiscriminately and ineptly borne along by the driving forces of his inclination, the simple animal of things and conditions, yet presently he puts a check upon his motivations and, rather than being controlled, starts to control.

2. Self-investigation. Having noticed the inclinations of the psyche, they are then firmly inspected and are put through an inflexible course of the investigation. The underhanded

propensities (those that produce difficult outcomes) are isolated from the great propensities (those that produce serene outcomes); and the different inclinations, with the specific activities they produce, and the unequivocal outcomes which perpetually spring from these activities, are continuously gotten a handle on by the comprehension, which is finally empowered to follow them in their quick and unobtrusive transaction and significant consequences. It is a course of verifying, and, for the searcher, a time of being verified.

3. Change. At this point, the useful understudy of things divine has obviously before him each inclination and part of his temperament, down to the most profound promptings of his brain, and the most inconspicuous intentions of his heart. There isn't a spot or corner left, that he has not investigated and enlightened with the radiance of self-assessment.

He knows about each feeble and egotistical point, major areas of strength for each high-minded quality. It is viewed as the level of intelligence to have the option to see ourselves as others see us, however, the specialist of restraint goes a long way past this: he not just sees himself as others see him, he sees himself as he is. Consequently, standing up close and personal with himself, not endeavoring to stow away from any mystery issue; done shielding himself with lovely blandishments; neither misjudging nor misrepresenting himself or his powers, and not any more reviled with self-acclaim or self-indulgence, he sees the full greatness of the assignment which lies before him; sees sincerely ahead the levels of discretion, and knows how work he needs to contact them.

He is at this point not in that frame of mind of disarray,

however, has acquired a brief look at the regulations which work in the realm of thought, and he presently starts to change his psyche as per those regulations.

This is a course of weeding, filtering, and purifying. As the rancher weeds, cleans, and readies the ground for his yields, so the understudy eliminates the weeds of evil from his brain, scrubs, and filters it preliminary to planting the seeds of equitable activities which will deliver the reap of a very much arranged life.

4. Righteousness. Having changed his contemplations and deeds to those minor regulations which work in mental exercises in the development of agony and delight, turmoil and harmony, distress and joy, he presently sees that there is engaged with those regulations one Great Central Law which, similar to the law of attractive energy in the regular world, is preeminent in the realm of the psyche; a regulation to which all considerations and deeds are compliant, and by which they are managed and kept in their legitimate circle.

This is the law of Justice or Righteousness, which is widespread and incomparable. To this regulation, he presently adjusts. Rather than thinking and acting aimlessly, as nature is invigorated and engaged by outward things, he subordinates his considerations and deeds to this focal standard. He no longer does demonstrations from himself, yet makes the wisest decision — what is all around and endlessly right. He is at this point not the contemptible slave of his inclination and conditions, he is the expert of his temperament and conditions.

He is not generally conveyed here and yonder on the powers of his psyche; he controls and guides those powers to the achievement of his motivations. In this way, having his temperament in charge and coercion, not thinking contemplations nor carrying out things which go against the exemplary regulation, and which, subsequently, that regulation repeals with torment and rout, he transcends the territory of transgression and distress, obliviousness and uncertainty, and is solid, quiet, and tranquil.

5. Pure Knowledge. By thinking right and acting right, he demonstrates, by experience, the presence of the heavenly regulation on which the brain is outlined, and which is the directing and binding together standard in every human undertaking and occasion, whether individual or public. Accordingly, by idealizing himself indiscretion, he gains divine information; he arrives where it could be said to describe him, as the regular researcher, that he knows.

He has dominated the study of restraint and has delivered information once again from obliviousness, requests out of disarray. He has obtained that information on self which incorporates information on all men; that information on one's daily routine which embraces information on all experience — concerning all personalities are a similar basically (contrasting just in degree), are outlined upon a similar regulation; and similar considerations and acts, by at all singular they are fashioned, will constantly create similar outcomes.

Be that as it may, this heavenly and harmony presenting information, as on account of the regular researcher, isn't acquired for a single's self; for on the off chance that this was thus, the point of development would be baffled, and it isn't in that frame of mind of things to miss the mark regarding maturing and achievement; and, without a doubt, he who remembered to acquire this information exclusively for his bliss would most definitely fizzle.

In this way, past the fifth step of Pure Knowledge, there is an, even more, one of Wisdom, which is the right use of the information gained; the spilling out upon the world, unselfishly and without spell, the consequence of one's works, hence speeding up progress and elevating mankind. It could be said to describe men who have not returned to their tendency to control and decontaminate it, that they can't recognize great and detestable, good and bad. They reach after those things which they think

will give them joy, and attempt to keep away from those things which they accept will cause them torment.

The wellspring of their activities is self, and they just find right horrendously and in a fragmentary manner, by occasionally going through serious sufferings, and lashings of soul. In any case, he who rehearses restraint, going through the five cycles, which are five phases of development, gains that information that empowers him to act from the ethical regulation which supports the universe. He knows great and underhanded, good and bad, and, in this manner knowing them, lives as per great and right. He never again needs to consider what is wonderful for sure is upsetting, however, makes the wisest decision; his temperament is as one with his still, small voice, and there is no regret; his psyche is as one with the Great Law, and there is not any more affliction and sin; for him, evil is finished, and great is with everything taken into account.

CAUSE AND EFFECT IN HUMAN CONDUCT

It is a saying among the researchers that each impact is connected with a reason. Apply this to the domain of human lead, and there is uncovered the guideline of Justice. Each researcher knows (and presently all men accept) that ideal agreement wins all through each piece of the actual universe, from the spot of residue to the best sun. Wherever there is a choice change. In the sidereal universe, with its large number of suns moving gloriously through space and conveying with them their particular frameworks of rotating planets, its tremendous cloud, its oceans of meteors, and its immense multitude of comets going through illimitable space with unfathomable speed, amazing request wins; and once more, in the normal world, with its countless parts of life, and its boundless assortment of structures, there are the characterized restrictions of explicit regulations, through the activity of which all disarray is stayed away from, and solidarity and concordance unceasingly get.

On the off chance that this widespread congruity could be randomly broken, even in one little specific, the universe would fail to be; there could be no universe, yet just general tumult. Nor might it at any point be conceivable in such a vast expanse of regulation that there ought to exist any private power which is above, outside, and prevalent too, such regulation as in it can oppose it, or put it away; for at all creatures exist, whether they be men or divine beings, they exist by the goodness of such regulation; and the most elevated, best, and savvies among all creatures would show his more noteworthy insight by his more complete submission to that regulation which is savvier than shrewdness, and than which nothing more wonderful could be contrived.

All things, whether apparent or undetectable, are docile too, and fall inside the extent of, this boundless and timeless law of causation. As everything is seen comply with it, so everything inconspicuous — the considerations and deeds of men, whether mysterious or open — can't get away from it.

"Do well, it recompenseth; treat one terribly, The equivalent retaliation should be made."

Wonderful equity maintains the universe; amazing equity controls human existence and direction. Every one of the changing states of life, as they get in this present reality, is the aftereffect of this regulation responding to human direction. Man can (and does) pick what causes he will set inactivity, yet he can't change the idea of impacts; he can choose what considerations he will think, and what deeds he will do, however, he has no control over

the consequences of those considerations and deeds; these are directed by the overruling regulation.

Man has all ability to act, however his power closes with the demonstration committed. The aftereffect of the demonstration can't be modified, abrogated, or got away; it is unavoidable. Detestable contemplations and deeds produce states of anguish; great considerations and deeds decide states of blessedness. Along with these lines, labor supply is restricted, and his blessedness or not set in stone by his direction. To know this reality renders life straightforward, plain, and undeniable; every one of the abnormal ways is fixed, the levels of intelligence are uncovered, and the entryway to salvation from malicious and enduring is seen and placed.

Life might be compared to a total in math. It is bewilderingly troublesome and complex to the student who has not yet gotten a handle on the way into its right arrangement, yet whenever this is seen and laid hold of, it becomes however amazingly straightforward as it seemed to be previously significantly puzzling. A few thought of this general effortlessness and intricacy of life might be gotten a handle on by completely perceiving and understanding the way that, while there are scores, and maybe hundreds, of manners by which a total might be fouled up, there is just a single way by which it tends to be done well, and that when that correct way is viewed the student knows it as the right; his perplexity disappears, and he realizes that he has dominated the issue.

It is the case that the student while doing his total mistakenly, may (and much of the time does) think he has done it accurately, however, he doesn't know; his perplexity is still there, and assuming he is a sincere and able understudy, he will perceive his blunder when it is brought up by the instructor. So throughout everyday life, men might think they are living properly while they are proceeding, through obliviousness, to live wrongly; however, the presence of uncertainty, perplexity, and misery are certain signs that the correct way has not yet been found.

There are silly and indiscreet understudies who might want to pass a total right before they have procured genuine information on figures, however, the eye and expertise of the instructor rapidly identify and uncover the deception. So in life, there can be no distorting of results; the eye of the Great Law uncovers and uncovered. Two times five will make ten to all forever, and no measure of obliviousness, idiocy, or dream can bring the outcome up to eleven.

If one takes a gander at a piece of fabric, he considers it to be a piece of material, yet on the off chance that he goes further and asks into its production, and looks at it intently and mindfully, he sees that it is made out of a blend of individual strings, and that, while every one of the strings is related, each string seeks after its particular manner all through, never-ending up being mistaken for its sister string. It is this whole shortfall of disarray between the specific strings which is the completed work of a piece of fabric; any discordant blending of the string would bring about a heap of waste or a pointless cloth.

Life resembles a piece of material, and the strings of which it is created are individual lives. The strings, while being related, are not perplexed by one with the other. Each follows its course. Every individual endures and partakes in the fallouts of his deeds, and not of the deeds of another. The course of each is basic and unequivocal; the entire shaping a muddled, yet agreeable, a mix of successions. There are activity and response, deed and result, circumstances and logical results, and the offsetting, outcome, and impact are generally in careful proportion with the initiatory motivation.

A tough and palatable piece of fabric can't be produced using trashy material, and the strings of childish considerations and terrible deeds won't deliver a valuable and wonderful life — a day-to-day existence that will wear well, and bear close review. Each man makes or damages his own life; it isn't made or defaced by his neighbor, or by anything outer to himself. Each thought he thinks, every deed he does is one more string — disgraceful or authentic — woven into the article of clothing of his life, and as he makes the article of clothing so should he wear it. He isn't answerable for his neighbor's deeds; he isn't the caretaker of his neighbor's activities; he is mindful just of his deeds; he is the overseer of his own decisions.

The "issue of wickedness" stays alive in a man's malevolent deeds, and it is settled when those deeds are refined. Says Rousseau:

"Man, look for as of now not the beginning of insidiousness; thou thyself workmanship its starting point." The impact can never be separated from the cause; it can never be of an alternate sort from the cause. Emerson says: "Equity isn't delayed; an ideal value changes the equilibrium in all pieces of life."

Furthermore, there is a significant sense wherein circumstances and logical results are concurrent and structured in one wonderful entirety. In this way, upon the moment that a man thinks, say, a brutal idea, or carries out a savage thing, that equivalent moment he has harmed his psyche; he isn't a similar man he was in the last moment; he is somewhat viler and somewhat more troubled, and various such progressive contemplations and deeds would deliver a horrible and pitiable man. The same thing applies to going against the norm — the reasoning of a sort thought, or carrying out a benevolent thing — a quick honorability and satisfaction go to it; the man is superior to he was previously, and various such deeds would deliver an extraordinary and merry soul.

Subsequently individual human direct decides, by the flawless law of circumstances and logical results, individual legitimacy or negative mark, individual significance or unpleasantness, individual bliss or horror. A man's thought process, that he does; what he does, that he is. Assuming he is confused, despondent, fretful, or pathetic, let him seek himself, for there and no place else is the wellspring of all his difficulty

TRAINING OF THE WILL

Without the strength of the brain, nothing deserving of achievement should be possible, and the development of that immovability and steadiness of character which is generally called "resolution" is one of the chief obligations of man, for its ownership is fundamental to both his worldly and everlasting prosperity. Fixedness of direction is at the base of every single fruitful exertion, whether in things common or otherworldly, and without it, a man can't be in any case than pitiable, and reliant upon others for that help which ought to be found inside himself.

The secret which has been tossed around the subject of the development of the will by the people who promote to sell "mysterious exhortation" regarding this situation for such countless dollars, ought to be stayed away from and dissipated, in vain could be additionally taken out from mystery and secret than the reasonable strategies by which alone strength of will can be created.

The genuine way of will development is just to be found in the normal day-to-day existence of the individual, thus self-evident and straightforward is it that the larger part, searching for something confounded and puzzling, passes it by inconspicuous.

A little consistent idea will before long persuade a man that he can't be both powerless and solid while, he can't foster a more grounded will while staying a captive to frail guilty pleasures, and that, consequently, the immediate and best way to that more noteworthy strength is to pounce upon and vanquish his shortcomings. Every one of the means for the development of the will is as of now close by in the psyche and life of the individual; they live in the feeble side of his personality, by going after and vanquishing the important strength of will be created. He who has prevailed with regards to getting a handle on this straightforward, primer truth, will see that the entire study of will development is encapsulated in the accompanying seven standards:

1. Break off unfortunate behavior patterns.

2. Form beneficial routines.

3. Give conscientious consideration regarding the obligation of the current second.

    4. Do enthusiastically, and without a moment's delay, whatever must be finished.

5. Live by rule.

6. Control the tongue.
7. Control the brain.

Any individual who sincerely ponders upon, and perseveringly rehearses, the above rules, won't neglect to foster that immaculateness of direction and force of will which will empower him to effectively adapt to each trouble, and pass victoriously through each crisis.

It will be seen that the initial step is the ending away from vices. This is no simple assignment. It requests the investing of incredible amounts of energy or a progression of endeavors, and it is by such endeavors that the will can alone be strengthened and braced. If one won't venture out, he can't increment in that frame of mind, by submitting to a negative behavior pattern, given the quick joy which it bears, one relinquishes the option to govern over himself and is up to this point a feeble slave. He who accordingly keeps away from self-control, and looks about for some "mysterious insider facts" for acquiring resolve at the use of next to zero exertion from him, is deceiving himself and is debilitating the determination which he as of now has.

The expanded strength of will which is acquired by progress in defeating persistent vices empowers one to start beneficial routines; for, while the vanquishing of an unfortunate behavior pattern requires simply strength of direction, the shaping of another one requires the clever heading of direction. To do this, a man should be intellectually dynamic and lively and should keep a steady watch on himself. As a man prevails with regards to culminating himself in the subsequent rule, it won't be extremely challenging for him to notice the third, that of focusing on the obligation of the current second.

Carefulness is a stage in the improvement of the will which can't be ignored. Slipshod work means that shortcoming.

Flawlessness ought to be focused on, even in the littlest undertaking. By not isolating the brain, however focusing on each different undertaking as it introduces itself, singleness of direction and extreme convergence of psyche are step by step acquired — two mental powers which give weight and worth to character and give rest and pleasure to their holder.

The fourth decision — that of doing enthusiastically, and on the double, whatever must be finished — is similarly significant. Inaction and a solid will can't go together, and lingering is a complete obstruction to the securing of deliberate activity. Nothing to be "put off" until some other time, not in any event, for a couple of moments. That which should be done now ought to be done at this point. This appears to be a seemingly insignificant detail, however, it is of broad significance. It prompts strength, achievement, and harmony.

The one who is to show a developed will should likewise live by specific fixed rules. He should not aimlessly satisfy his interests and motivations, however, should school them to comply. He ought to live as per standard, and not as indicated by energy.

He ought to choose what he will eat and drink and wear, and what he won't eat and drink and wear; the number of suppers each day he will have, and at what times he will have them; at what time he will hit the sack, and at what time get up. He ought to make rules for the right administration of his direct in each branch of his life, and ought to strictly comply with them. To live freely and unpredictably, eating and drinking and erotically revealing available no matter what to craving and tendency is to be a simple creature and not a man with will and reason.

The monster in man should be scourged and restrained

and brought into coercion, and this must be would via preparing the care and life on specific fixed rules of the right direction. The holy person achieves blessedness by not disregarding his promises, and the one who lives as per great and fixed rules, areas of strength for achieving his motivation.

The 6th rule, that of controlling the tongue, should be rehearsed until one has the ideal order of his discourse, so he doesn't articulate anything in touchiness, outrage, peevishness, or with a detestable plan. The man's areas of strength for of doesn't permit his tongue to run neglectfully and without checking.

This large number of six guidelines, if loyally rehearsed, will pave the way to the seventh, which is the most significant of all — to be specific, properly controlling the psyche. Restraint is the most fundamental thing throughout everyday life, yet least got it; yet he who persistently rehearses the principles thus set down, acquiring them into demand every one of his methodologies and endeavors, will learn, by his insight and endeavors, how to control and prepare his mind, and to procure in this manner the preeminent crown of masculinity — the crown of an impeccably ready will.

A grateful person is always happy no matter a day or two. He finds happiness in every bit. He is always confident. Sometimes people get sick and het panic about life and think they are losing everything and not being given what they deserve but a grateful person never thinks this way he is always grateful for not having the worse sickness and at least given a life better than soo many out there. A day in a grateful person's life may have ups and downs but they always try to encourage themselves by making a thought process that it could've been worse but it's not.

They tend to have a healthy mind and healthy relationships so are free from depression, stress, etc. No matter what happens in a day they don't make that one bad page of their life's book become a whole bad book itself. They start recognizing everything that happens good or bad happens for a reason and will always profit them in one way or the other.

*"Everything we do should be a result of our gratitude for
what God has done for us."*

Lauryn Hill

CHAPTER V

Live Gratefully

When you foster a disposition of an earnest demeanor for all the gifts you get, this releases the power for you to get much more than you now have. Having the sensation of gratitude implies underestimating nothing and expressing gratefulness about the overflow in life that you have gotten. Gratitude finds a place with overflow in different angles. As a renowned author says, "Many individuals are caught in the condition of neediness by having an absence of gratitude." Abundance generally goes with gratitude since we can constantly draw in incredible abundance as well as overflow with the force of gratitude. How It Fits "much obliged" signifies a ton of things and these are the absolute best words that you need to say for simply everything. Many individuals today are asking why their life isn't exactly bountiful, why numerous beneficial things don't occur to them, and for what reason aren't they cheerful. There is a great deal of "whys".

Many individuals are carrying on with daily existence loaded with grievances. This is one of the primary purposes for your absence of overflow throughout everyday life. Assuming you generally see things adversely, you won't ever see the value in the beneficial things you have and the gift you get. When you begin viewing everything in your life as a gift and as beneficial things to be appreciative of, then your life will become significant and you will be cheerful. Your feeling of gratitude will bring the incredible overflow that you have been longing for. How you see life, and how you contemplate the things around you, have an immense effect on how bountiful you are a major part of your life today. The sensation of gratitude is truly strong and it is a fundamental piece of your life that can carry you to the things you need. At the point when you begin looking and zeroing in your energy on being genuinely appreciative, you get genuine overflow in your life. Life is brimming with favors. It is loaded up with a ton of things that you want and you want. We super confuse it with our negative idea designs. When you open your eyes to the best things around you and for every one of the straightforward things that can be perfect for you, you can perceive how rich you are and how plentiful your life truly is. Gratitude generally finds a place with overflow. The essential key to acquiring genuine overflow in life is through figuring out how to become appreciative even in however you are living in a dissatisfied world.

Deciding What To Be Grateful For

There are a lot of things around us to be thankful for; it's simply an issue of valuing the gift you get and recognizing how favored you are for having them. Teaching yourself about the sensation of demeanor implies underestimating nothing and giving worth to whatever you gang. Practice the demeanor of never putting off n activity or the word for the declaration of your gratitude. Numerous people will quite often underestimate the things that are available in their lives. There is a gratitude practice teaching us to envision losing not many of the things that you are underestimating today, for example, your family, your home, as well as your capacity to hear and see, to walk, or simply whatever is as of now giving you solace. Envision losing them and afterward envision that you are getting every one of them back each day. Figure how appreciative you would be at the point at which it works out and when everyone has rewarded you. Concluding Starting finding satisfaction even in those little things you gangs as opposed to waiting for perfect and huge accomplishments like landing position advancement, having a child, or getting hitched. There are a ton of things to be appreciative of. At the point when you wake in the first part of the day, be appreciative of the existence you have for one more day. Your joy generally relies heavily on how you view life itself and how you see your life today. Assuming you start to feel that there are considerably more things to be thankful for, you will perceive the way blissful your life will is. To completely see the value throughout everyday life and your reality, you must be truly careful about even those easily overlooked details around you. A spread that zooms around you that encourages you, the food on your table, your great wellbeing - these things may be exceptionally basic for you, yet assuming you start to recognize them as favors, your life will become more joyful. Use gratitude to direct you in placing things in their right viewpoint. Assuming everything around you appears to be off-base, and on the off chance that things don't go how you believe they should be, remember that each issue and trouble conveys inside it the seeds of a more prominent advantage. At the point when you are confronting any test in your life and when you are notwithstanding incredible misfortune, simply get some information about the beneficial things that you can get from it. Comprehend how you can profit from a specific circumstance. Whenever you start to see the value throughout everyday life and, surprisingly, the little things that might happen to you, you likewise start to make the existence of satisfaction, agreement, happiness, and rapture. Assuming you are encountering a tough spot, never consider it weight or discipline. Be grateful about the preliminaries that you are confronting because they can make you significantly more grounded. Be appreciative of your concerns since they make you a superior person.

How Gratitude Works With Abundance

Gratitude is something that requires no clarification; everybody knows how to become appreciative. That being said, gratitude is tied in with valuing all that you get and remembering your good fortune. Nonetheless, many individuals don't know that gratitude incredible works with overflow. Gratitude and overflow go commonly. Even though you may not know it, but rather it is a fact that your sensation of gratitude generally brings overflow. This truly brings you much a greater amount of what you truly appreciate. How It Works Gratitude speeds along with the indications of your desired things. Gratitude draws in what you truly care about. As the general law of Attraction uncovers, we can draw into our lives the things that we center around and we contemplate. Presently, when you're intentionally mindful of the things you get and you are thankful for getting them, you're likewise zeroing in obviously on those that you need throughout everyday life and you are drawing in considerably a greater amount of those things to your life. You need to recall that gratitude is truly strong. This is a truly compelling close-to-home energy that one should have the option to project in the way of showing their needs throughout everyday life. Assuming that you are appreciative of the things you get and the gifts in your day-to-day existence, you are drawing in overflow. Giving accentuation to a sensation of gratitude towards anything that life offers you quickly brings you into a lively arrangement having an expanded overflow. Gratitude truly keeps you stay associated with incredible power. Additionally, the more you learn and work on being grateful and appreciative, there will be more considered designs genuine gratitude that you work in your psyche. In the long run, you are resounding with a more significant level of energy and have the option to draw in additional beneficial things into your life. Gratitude impeccably works with acquiring incredible overflow. On the off chance that you're in an ardent gratitude expression, your vibrational reverberation is all the more remarkable. You start to resound, consequently, you project a considerably higher vibrational recurrence that precisely draws in you to those circumstances, conditions, and occasions that you need. Assuming you are in the condition of gratitude, you start to remember you're a good fortune. You are starting to decide the beneficial things around you and you ignore the negativities encompassing you. Assuming that you start to be content and satisfied with anything you have throughout everyday life, you effectively recognize even the basic gifts you get. With this, you are not exclusively being plentiful transiently with the wealth you need, however, you are likewise ready to get an astonishing gift outside your ability to understand. Your life becomes more joyful, you enjoy the harmony of the psyche, and you work on the nature of your life - which fills in as the best overflow you can have in your life.

Getting In The Right Mindset

Having the right mentality implies viewing something as thankful for in each trouble. If you have a set perspective about existence and the things around you, you can see the open door behind each issue. Assuming you can recognize the beneficial things in your day-to-day existence amid variety, you have the right outlook that will lead you towards a cheerful life. Despite hardships and in the present sinking economy, it is truly challenging for us to stay thankful and appreciative. When you feel overpowered and worried, it is once in a while difficult to come by motivations to become appreciative. It is the case that the majority of the time, finding the positive qualities in a tough spot can truly be testing. In any case, the extraordinary advantages of keeping up with appreciation and veritable gratitude regardless of what is happening around you, are worth investigating. Having the right attitude about being thankful can extraordinarily change your life.

Every one of us has our favors throughout everyday life. Despite what your identity is, where you came from, and for sure what you are going through, you generally have favors in your day-to-day existence that you can be appreciative of. The main test here is to teach yourself to give an accentuation on gratitude and quest for some reasons for you to show appreciation. Practice to Acknowledge the Good If you are a sort of individual who isn't exactly thankful, well this is the best time for you to foster your new propensity. This propensity is tied in with looking for something to be appreciative of about each circumstance, an experience that you experience, or an individual. In each tough spot that you experience, this can truly be troublesome, however assuming you can foster this propensity, you can see tremendous changes in your day-to-day existence and how you view life itself. You simply need to buckle down in tracking down a little piece of jewel in an enormous rough mountain. You can likewise offer gratitude for a caring relationship with your accomplice and family, your great well-being, and those positive results in different circumstances.

Gratitude is truly strong and being completely mindful of the endowments you get can tremendously affect your life. If you are loaded up with gratefulness and appreciation, this changes your world's dynamic. Offer appreciation and thanks to those individuals around you. Assuming something great happen to you, regardless of how large or little it is, be grateful that it works out. Assuming you get into the right mentality about having a sensation of gratitude towards others and every circumstance, you will likewise feel better about yourself. You will have an alternate point of view about existence and you will see the world as something delightful. It is astounding how a positive activity can make such a lot of progress in the existence of an individual. Recognizing the extraordinary force of disposition is one of the main things today that make an incredible impact on one's life. In bright substantial ways, the facts confirm that gratitude can make your life far and away superior.

The Difference Between Positive And Negative Mindsets
In Gratitude Your perspective about gratitude, whether positive or negative, can make various effects on your day-to-day existence. There are extraordinary contrasts between a certain and negative mentality in gratitude and anything that your perspective about it can roll out huge improvements in your life. Gratitude generally matters. On the off chance that you have a negative mentality in gratitude, you will see trouble in every open door, yet assuming you have a positive outlook in gratitude, you can see extraordinary open doors in every trouble. The Good And The Bad Negative Mindset in Gratitude All individuals get favors - in any capacity or any structure. The issue is that the vast majority don't actually see the value in them

or even underestimate these favors. Individuals frequently neglect to offer ordinary gratitude for what they previously acquired. These days, it is normally simpler to slip into the negative mentality and spotlight inclining further toward your greater objectives for the future and to those things that you presently can't seem to accomplish. Indeed, nothing bad can be said about reaching skyward and looking upwards and onwards; this is essential for human instinct. Notwithstanding, the issue with it is that you beginning to fail to remember the ongoing favors that you are acquiring. Assuming you have a negative outlook on gratitude, you won't thoroughly be blissful. Assuming you begin underestimating the things that you as of now have in light of your greater targets, you will become disappointed and you will acquire genuine bliss, particularly assuming you are still distant from your goals. Assuming you can perceive even the basic things around you while intending to arrive at your objective, there is an incredible distinction between these two. You can go for the gold while recognizing the things you now have today. Good Mindset in Gratitude The words you express and the inclination you express ordinary extraordinarily influence your life. On the off chance that you are acquiring extraordinary euphoria and overflow throughout everyday life, it is likewise a result of your opinion on the things around you and the words you express. Assuming that you have a positive attitude in gratitude, you give more appreciation to even the littlest things around you, and along these lines, you become much more joyful. How you contemplate gratitude and your disposition towards the things around you have incredible effects on your day-to-day existence. Remember that positive energy given out will ultimately get back with incredible prizes. How you ponder gratitude reflects in the manner in which you see life. Recall that gratitude is your most significant association with God, communicating your appreciation for the beneficial things in your day-to-day existence and consequently, getting something else for you to be grateful for. Give appreciation to everything around you and you will likewise draw in delight and overflow in your life.

Transforming Bad Days Into Gratitude Days
Whenever things don't turn out well for us and when everything around us appears to self-destruct, the last thing that we can imagine is to be grateful. Whenever we are confronting hardships, everything we do is whine and inquire as to why terrible things are occurring to us. Transforming awful days into gratitude days is difficult for some individuals, yet it is conceivable all the time. Work on Counting your Blessings - Not every one of your Troubles People invest the vast majority of their energy mourning about their difficulties, whining about the challenges they experience and the ill effects that they never again care about the gifts that they have gotten. At the point when looking at challenges, individuals truly will quite often fail to remember what they have and the beneficial things in their day-to-day existence. Individuals are welcome to begin remembering their good fortune, even name them individually and they will simply be astonished about those astounding things that God had done in their lives. At the point when looking at preliminaries and difficulties, remember you're good fortune and you will likewise see that your heart will develop heartily with many sensations of gratitude as well as wonderful sensations of satisfaction and harmony. Take a gander at the Brighter Side of Every Situation If you experience issues and challenges at work,

be more appreciative that you have your work. If you are confronting difficulties throughout everyday life, be more thankful for these moves because of them, your life isn't exhausting. Assuming you are confronting preliminaries in your day-to-day existence today, be appreciative that these can invigorate you much conquer more preliminaries later on. Value your difficulties in life that can help you learn and be a more grounded individual. To say that we are appreciative doesn't imply that everything in your life is awesome; it just implies that you know about the entirety of your endowments disregarding the difficulties that you are encountering. Assuming you stay furious, steamed, and baffled since you are having a downright terrible day, that won't change anything. That would compound the situation, truth be told. Bringing appreciation during these times can light up your day as well as others. Getting what you need isn't the main justification for you to be thankful, some of the time, your appreciation in life turns out to be significantly more important when you figure out how to be grateful amid difficulties and troubles. Assuming you are in a tough spot, rather than abhorring the world for giving you such an issue, consider the advantage that you can profit from it. Contemplate the things that you can acquire from this present circumstance and through this, you will turn out to be more enlivened to beat the tough spot you are into. Continuously search for something to be thankful for in each terrible day you face. Likewise, it is smarter to comprehend the explanation you are in such circumstances and consider the best things that you can get from it. On the off chance that you figure out how to turn out to be more thankful and content with each circumstance you are in, you can become more joyful in your life. Continuously be thankful that you don't as of now have everything that you need since, in such a case that you did, there will be something else to anticipate. Be more appreciative for each troublesome satiation you are into because, in those times, you can develop.

How Gratitude Can Change What you Attract

Being thankful in any sort of circumstance is a solid drawing in force. Gratitude diminishes cynicism, assists individuals with learning, further develops connections and above all, gratitude draws in the things that you need. This is an extraordinary and strong power that can change what one can draw in. The Great Power of Gratitude Once you find things you appreciate and you begin giving accentuation on the things you are grateful for, you can constantly draw in them. As you begin flooding your psyche with gratitude or appreciation, you draw in a greater amount of those that you need. Assuming you are in a condition of gratitude, you are likewise in a high energy vibration fundamental in drawing in additional things that you can be appreciative of. There will likewise be more things that will mysteriously come to you - things that are brought into you by your concentration and incredible sensations of gratitude. Getting What You Want To just A feeling of bliss draws in the states of satisfaction and similarly, your sensation of appreciation draws in additional things that you can be thankful for. The Universal Law of Attraction uncovers that one will draw into their life the things that they center around and ponder. If you offer your thanks for something, you are completely mindful of that gift. In this situation, you're giving more spotlight on the things that you truly need throughout everyday life and consequently, you are drawing in a greater amount of these things into your own life. Likewise, gratitude makes your desired things more substantial and fills in as a genuine part of your world. The more genuine and substantial your cravings are, the more you will give an incredible spotlight on them. That being said, gratitude is truly strong. It can determine issues, works on your life, and helps you learn and draw in your desired things. This can enormously change what you draw in because the more mindful you are about the favors and beneficial things you get, you give more clarity of mind to it by communicating your appreciation. This will thusly empower you to draw in certain energies to acquire what you need. Gratitude truly matters. It doesn't just permit us to acquire what we need yet it additionally prompts positive activities. At the point when one feels appreciative of the benevolence displayed by an individual, one might be bound to offer grace to the individual consequently. This is then truly accommodating in making great associations with others. With numerous gifts that you can take benefit from appreciation and expressing gratefulness for the things you get, there is not a great explanation for you not to the training the mentality of gratitude. This won't just draw in beneficial things on your life yet on the existences of others also

Gratitude releases life's completion. Carrying on with a daily existence brimming with gratitude can constantly wipe the slate clean. There are a ton of benefits that you can imagine once you begin showing your gratitude towards others. Additionally, appreciating your life brings incredible advantages that can build the nature of your life.

The Differences in Advantage of Gratitude
Gratitude can help us to remember the positive and incredible things in our lives. It can satisfy us, knowing that

in each tough spot that we are confronting, there are still a lot of things to be appreciative of. Assuming you practice a demeanor of gratitude, you can continuously transform your awful days into great days. Gratitude is additionally truly beneficial because it can help us to remember what is significant. It is difficult to whimper or grumble about a few easily overlooked details once you begin giving things that you are alive today and sound. It is likewise hard to be overpowered or worried about your over-covering bills once you are blissful and appreciative that you have a home with your loved ones. Gratitude permits us to see the world from a wonderful point of view. It empowers us to see each tough spot as something that will invigorate us and our ability to move forward and carry on with a cheerful and bright life. The act of gratitude can expand our degree of joy and work on the nature of our life. Whenever you begin seeing the world as a delightful spot for you to learn, work on yourself and become more grounded, your life turns out to be more significant. When you can perceive the things that you should be grateful for, you will likewise find that you are beginning to see the value in straightforward things and delights that you previously underestimated. Gratitude is something that ought not to be just a response to get what you need or draw in what you want, yet it should be something that can assist you with recognizing those seemingly insignificant details around you. This must likewise be something that can assist you with continually looking for the great however undesirable circumstances might occur. The vast majority of the time, while discussing negative circumstances, we accept that it is unsafe, miserable, troublesome, and, surprisingly, upsetting. Notwithstanding, assuming that you have a demeanor of gratitude, you can think emphatically in each bad circumstance. You investigate each detail and attempt to view something as appreciative. You accept that there is something worth being thankful for in each tough spot and issues are viewed as any open doors to work on yourself and to develop. Hindrance of Gratitude With the said extraordinary benefits of gratitude, one could barely find anything off-base about showing your gratitude and appreciation to each circumstance and each individual. Gratitude is something that will continuously bring harmony, satisfaction, and bliss to individuals. It can decrease negativities, work on all connections, draw in what your heart wants, and give joy to one's life. Gratitude is free. It requires no cash and a tiny bit of time so there is not any justification for anybody to show the amount they value an individual or express gratefulness to any circumstance they are in. With the positive attributes of gratitude, it is truly difficult for anybody to track down any weakness about it.

Gratitude is a strong inclination. It reveals the completion of one's life and it can transform negative things into something wonderful. Gratitude can transform tumult into request, forswearing to acknowledgment and disarray into clearness. It can turn a house into a home, an alien into a companion and it makes an everyday routine worth experiencing. Gratitude should not exclusively be an articulation after you have gotten something you need; however, it should likewise be something that can assist you with looking for chances to be appreciative during disagreeable circumstances. Presently, begin bringing the mentality of gratitude into your encounters, and instead of trusting that good results, you will feel appreciative. Amid tough spots, view something as appreciative. Everything occurs for an explanation and in each issue, there is continuously something great that you can get. If you have been whining about the sort of life you have, this is the ideal opportunity to take a delay, think, and search for the beneficial things in anything circumstance you are in. Begin carrying on with an existence of gratitude. If you haven't said "much obliged" to a companion in light of a straightforward tap when you are dealing with issues in your day-to-day existence, this is the ideal time for you to show your appreciation to the person in question. Be appreciative so that your capacity might see, hear, smell, talk, and walk. Count your endowments and you will surely be astonished about the number of favors you that have been getting all through your life. Talk about expressions of gratitude and perceive how you can draw in the things you need throughout everyday life. Perceive every one of your accomplishments and express gratefulness to yourself for keeping solid. Express gratefulness to your folks, a straightforward "card to say thanks" will do. Have you done something great to other people yet never got any badge of appreciation? Not even "bless your heart". Assuming you feel frustrated with that, contemplate how disheartened your folks are for not getting even an expression of gratitude for the lunch they pressed, things they purchased, and supper arranged for you. On the off chance that things don't turn out well for you, and you imagine that all in all nothing remains to be appreciative for, simply search for something great out of such circumstance. If you don't have everything that you need, then, at that point, be appreciative since, supposing that you do, there will be something else to anticipate. Be appreciative of every one of your blemishes since they give you a chance to work on more. Be appreciative of each challenge you face since it can fabricate your personality. Try not to surrender if you commit botches because your missteps will show you significant examples. Continuously be thankful. Show your gratitude to everybody and each circumstance and you will perceive the way it can change the nature of your life.

Let's dive into the most interesting & final topic, Destiny

"When we focus on our gratitude, the tide of disappointment goes out and the tide of love rushes in."

Kristin Armstrong

CHAPTER VI

A Day In The Life Of A Grateful Person
Shilpa Agrawal

I was born in a traditional Marwari family with four sisters & a brother!

Although My father was very loving & caring ..... but he never allowed wed us to wear western clothes & to go to a party, to movies, mingling with friends, especially opposite sex! Our daily routine used to be ..... going to school / junior college & back home !! But we use to enjoying at home ... Since we sisters were very close to each other & never felt any need for outside friendship !!

I was a very good student & I always dreamt of becoming a doctor one day !!

But my family married me off very early before I turned nineteen! I was just the 12th pass then!

Marriage was a new beginning .... but it came with a lot of responsibilities & expectations from all the members of my new family !!

The next few years were a very difficult period of my life! I could not cope with the pressure of being a wife, and daughter-in-law, in a traditional conservative combined family! although I was a very friendly, bubbly, cheerful girl At times I was a little inflexible, hot-headed, impulsive, use to get angry & irritated on small matters !!

My mother-in-law was a very assertive & strong-headed lady! She use to manage our family business without even being educated at all! She could only attend primary school! But over time due to her illness & old age (my husband was the youngest child), she has also become unpredictable & had developed some psychological problems!

We use to have a lot of fights over petty issues !!

At age of 20, I delivered a baby boy (We were young & had limited knowledge About family planning)!

I was barely coping with various pressure of married life & additional huge responsibility of motherhood without much support from my in-laws proved too much for me !!

At the age of 22, I tried to commit suicide by consuming a bottle of sleeping pills !! I thought that was the easiest way of getting rid of all my problems !!

That day was Sunday ...... Akash was at home ....he immediately took me to the hospital & somehow my life was saved but I was hospitalized for a week........ !!!

Akash who till now was a mute spectator to all the happening at home was shattered !!

He sensed .....things have changed forever .... Some drastic changes have to happen !!

During the week I was in the hospital, Akash had a detailed discussion with me & told me don't run away from the situation .... u r not a coward........do something creative in life .... u r born to excel !!!.

And ..these lines were the turning point in my life .... After that I never looked back and immediately I joined our family business !! with the motivation & guidance of my husband I grew in leaps and bounds as we complimented each other and become one plus one eleven, our business scaled to new heights !!

Myself joining business was Akash decision ...... As he understood that I being a very strong lady would be more successful as a professional / business lady rather than being a housewife in a combined Marwari family! I also realized seating at home I am getting frustrated doing routine work !!

Although Akash was very loving & protective as my father was ..... but especially after my suicide attempt, he become a more open-minded & very supportive husband, unlike a traditional Marwari husband !!!
After I joined the business, he started taking me to Jaycee club, rotary club, Vidarbha industries association, Vidarbha management association & many other association programs on self-development & business development ..
! He was always a very social person & was a member of many association & club-like rotary club of Nagpur !!!
It was this exposure that exposed me to the outside world socially & professionally !!

When I joined Akash furniture group it was running in losses. Initially, it took me a few years to completely have a grasp of business !! Initially, I use to come for 2/3 hrs per day ..... but slowly business world started fascinating me ...... I took a keen interest in our business & slowly with my effort & passion Akash furniture group became one of the most recognized & biggest furniture brands in central India.

As I started devoting more & more time ..... Slowly Akash took a back seat as he was always a very social person who loves to be very actively involved as an office-bearer of many social & trade organizations which used to consume most of his time daily !! Also since he was interested in shares trading, & property investment ... He use to devote a lot of time to that activity!!
he was an avid reader so he use to give a few hours a day reading about current affairs, business, psychology, etc !!
But he was always used to be on my side whenever I need His support, guidance, his vision, his strategies, etc !!!
After a few years in business, I used to devote 4 to 5 hrs & use to feel that I am doing enough as a women entrepreneur

but my perspective changed entirely when I visited China, Malaysia, Singapore & Thailand to study furniture industries & visit furniture exhibitions there! on seeing women entrepreneurs working very hard & rubbing shoulders with their male counterparts, I was further motivated to become a full-time women industrialist !!

! It has also inspired me to excel & become one of the top lady industrialists of India so that I can be a role model for other women & also inspires them to come into the industry & thus contribute toward India becoming a business & industrial superpower!

I am very proud & very humbly would like to say that now I am one of the very few lady industrialists in the whole of central India who is in full time into management & execution of hardcore business of manufacturing, wholesaling & retailing of consumer durable (A domain mostly managed by males)

I am happy to share that recently I got
* rotary vocational excellence award " by rotary international through the rotary club of Nagpur ..... a very prestigious award given to top achievers in the field of your chosen vocation (in my case entrepreneurship)!
* And to top it all ... I got one of the biggest awards in my life that are at the hand of then CM of Maharashtra Prithviraj Chavan ...." best lady industrialist of the region " !!

** also very recently I have been nominated by times of India for the Nagpur heroes award which will be given at hands of the honorable CM of Maharashtra Shri Devendra fadnavis on 12 Dec ! I am nominated for Nagpur heroes for my various achievements in the field of business, beauty pageants, promotion of women entrepreneurship, promotion & guidance for beauty pageants & also for getting selected for Mrs universe !!!

Today I am CEO of Akash furniture group consisting of Akash furnitech Pvt ltd (a 42000 sq feet state of art furniture industry at Hingna midc), Akash wholesale furniture mall (10000 sq feet furniture mall) & two showrooms at Nagpur !!!

I look after the entire production, sales & general administration of our group !!! I am managing about 100 skilled, unskilled & staff members !!! Most of them are women ..... as I feel women are better managers than men as they are multitaskers, more ethical, have more empathy towards others, have more patience & work harder than their male counterparts!!

Also, I want to promote women's entrepreneurship & I am very sure many of them in the future will start their industry.... may be small to start with !!

Now We are in the process of expanding our production facility to two lakh sq feet in next few years(construction of plant already started) & plan to supply all types of furniture across India & also exports !!!

my entrepreneurial journey was never easy ..... Since the furniture industry was male-dominated, I was the only woman entrepreneur it has !!

Also, it is a highly unorganized industry mostly managed by traditional very conservative male entrepreneurs !!

Most of the time I have to get work done from unskilled/ nonprofessional male subordinates which was at times very difficult for a lady as it use to bruise their male ego !!

many of my competitors when they were not able to compete with me professionally, ... use to spread rumors in the market that I am trying to get orders for furniture from various institutions using undue/unethical means of being a lady !! When I won a major furniture order competing with my close relative who was also our business competitor .... he accused me of getting this order by offering unethical favors women can offer ....and That day was one of the worst days in my life .... I cried the whole night and have decided to leave business & professional once and for all........ forever !!

Also during the same period, some of my customers tried to take undue advantage of me & also most of my relatives were not happy that the bahu of their family is working in the male-dominated industry !!

But again my shining light ... My pillar of strength...... Akash convinced me & told me Shilpa .... this is a male-dominated society! Any female who will try to enter this male-dominated field will have to initially face all these things !! He said in this world most the male is the same ...... they will try to take advantage of you, try to demoralize you ..... consider you as weak ..... But it is up to you to show them .... real strength of Indian married women & stand up & be counted !! He also told me it is Upto you .... how to make our reputation so that no one takes you for granted !!

During all this Akash stood behind me like a rock !! He said this is part & parcel of being in this competitive .... Dog eat dog world where survival of the fittest!

That again reenergized & reassured me & I never looked back !!

Today a 12-pass lady is visiting faculty to various MBA, BBA, and Engg colleges such IMT Katol, tirpude college, lad college & many more & professional organizations like VIA, TIE, VMA, etc!!

Regarding my participation in beauty pageants ....it all started in 2004 when Akash saw an advertisement in the newspaper & motivated me to participate in the Mrs. Nagpur contest!

I won Mrs. Nagpur 2004 & then also won Mr & Mrs. Nagpur contest along with Akash in 2005 !!

Then I participated in Gladrags Mrs. India & Mrs. India world contest but couldn't get selected for the finals !!

Then for the next 10 years, I got busy with my fast-growing business which demanded my full attention & time !!

Then in Sep 2015 .... Akash heard of Mrs. India's worldwide competition as one of her friends was participating in it ... ... He again motivated me to participate in it ....

Initially, I was very scared as it has been 10 yrs that I have participated in Gladrags Mrs. India !!

Also, I came to know that Majority of contestants in Mrs. India worldwide were from services (army, navy, airforce). Their family background in services bestowed them with confidence, poise, grace, talent, and risk-taking since their childhood !!

Many of them trained for beauty pageants for months from reputed international beauty pageant institutes like TIARA training institute Pune (which conducts courses for beauty pageants) !!

Many of them married recently & were participants of beauty pageants like miss India before marriage !!

But still, I somehow participated & manage to win Mrs. India's worldwide Mrs inspirational title!!

At Mrs. India worldwide Because of my performance in grooming, talent & other initial rounds ..... I was one of the top contenders & was expected to win the crown ....

But I couldn't .... And was told afterward... That top three positions were sold !!

I took that in my stride & again tried for Mrs. India globe

Where I won Mrs. India globe 1 st runner-up title (Indian married women from all over the globe were the participants)!

Again here all judges told me that they have given me the top position but the organizer gave the top position to somebody else Due to commercial reasons! It took it sportingly as by now I have understood........ " the law of average ..... You lose some. You win some but you have to keep trying !!

I am now selected to represent India in the most prestigious beauty contest for married women in the world which is Mrs universe which is going to happen in 2016 !!

Since many of my friends ask me why I participate in so many beauty pageants Here I would like to tell them ....participating in beauty pageants is not just about winning the title, name & or fame ....

It is much more !!!!

It is about meeting talented, interesting people, making friends with them, and learning from them !!
It is about the grooming you get ......
..... Exposure you get
..... The confidence you develop
& much more ..... !!

I would like more & more women of tier 2/3 cities like Nagpur to participate in these pageants & show they are equal .... if not better than their metro counterpart !!

.... And With this in mind, I am already guiding/ helping/mentoring more than 100 existing & would-be participants of Mrs. India / miss India contests from not only all over India but also from countries like Nigeria, Nepal, the USA, Europe, etc !!

I am very happy that ..... more than 25 to 30 of them would be participating in various Mrs. India / miss India contests in the next few months !!

I have already made a Whatsapp group of all interested (including Mrs. India, miss India & other beauty pageants) .... where I am interacting & sharing my experience, learning, & knowledge with them!

Also, every member of the group is sharing their learning, knowledge & experience for the benefit of all !!

Dance is my passion

I am happy to tell you that dance is also one of my passion & have won many dance contests at various levels !!

I was selected after many auditions for the final auditions of DID super mom organized by Zee tv in Mumbai but .... couldn't be selected for the final show on Zee tv !!

But I assure you that I will try till I am selected for finals which are shown on Zee tv as a dance reality show!

Many of my friends always ask me to open my dance academy looking at my skill & enthusiasm in teaching dance to them ..... which I keep on doing during our many dance fellowship Party at rotary club of Nagpur & also during various ladies sangeet functions during marriages of near & dear ones !!

One day I will like to open my dance academy!

My beauty & fitness regime!

I think for every woman of any age maintaining a fitness & beauty regime is important !! If we are physically & mentally fit then only we will be able to fulfill our multiple responsibilities and at the same time pursue our various passions !!

Beauty is one of the very important essences of womanhood, God has created every woman beautiful so we must maintain that virtue !!

I follow the fitness routine of alternating between running, gymming & yoga for at least one hour per day !! As I easily get bored by doing only one type of exercise !! to get maximum results, you have to keep on changing/ alternating between various types of exercise!!

Yoga I do to for flexibility, gym for toning, strengthening & running for losing fat !!

My beauty regime:--

To be very honest, I don't follow any beauty regime !! Only during grooming sessions in various pageants, I have learned a few makeup tips which I follow while going to parties & removing that makeup before going to bed !!

Apart from this, I don't believe in doing much for beauty !! I believe your inner beauty is much more important than external beauty !!

Also, I believe " you are what you eat & exercise " so if you eat healthily & stay healthy .... You will stay beautiful for ur entire life !!

Nagpur --

Nagpur is very close to my heart! Although I was born in Calcutta it was Nagpur that has given me my identity! It was Nagpur who has given me the Mrs. Nagpur title which today has motivated me to take part in Mrs universe !!

Nagpur because of its unique advantages of being a peaceful city, and very less traffic time has given me enough time to indulge in my various passions being an industrialist, dancer, beauty pageant participant & also doing a little bit of social work! It would have not been possible if I would have been in other metro cities !!

People here know each other & are very helpful as everybody has enough time which again helps women like me who have come up from difficult times !!

My stress buster

Being a professional married woman I have to give equal justice to my industry, family & also my social commitments !!

And they all have their timelines, which create a lot of stress !!

But over some time, I have learned to take this stress as an opportunity to improve my work by creating systems in my organization so that I am not needed for small work & decisions!! But all said and done you still have to go through stress occasionally! But my love for yoga, running & dancing where I get time to connect with my inner me & have a dialogue with myself is a great stress buster for me !! Guiding aspiring youngsters & women entrepreneurs is also a great stress buster for me !!

My son Aryan studies in a residential School in Panchgani & whenever he is on school holiday we go on family vacation & that vacation is also a great stress buster for me !!

Managing personal & professional life

Managing personal & professional life is one of the biggest challenges every woman has to face the world over !!

But I believe God has given every woman enough talent in form of multitasking, empathy, patience, etc to overcome this challenge !!

They only need some support & motivation which I received from my husband !!

If women are well supported by family or at least their hubby managing personal & professional life is not a big deal for them !!

In my case, my only son Aryan is in boarding school since he was in 5 the class! It was a conscious decision to make him independent & give him exposure to practical life! For most of the months, he is in boarding school so I don't have to devote much time to him !!

Since my joining of business although my small problems with my in-laws persist now I am mature enough to manage those issues as now I don't react impulsively to that issue but try to manage with a cool head & reasoning!

Creating a niche for myself in the business & pageant world without any education !!

A lot of people ask me especially when I interact with MBA, Engg students, and would-be entrepreneurs ..... how I can manage my business ... Where I have to manage accounts (both internal accounts & also various taxation issues), production, sales, marketing, transportation, human resources, etc all by myself especially since ours is an SME industry where we cannot afford to hire professionals for every function of management ????

I always tell them education is a must for everybody But Your .... main learning starts when you enter this very competitive " dog eat dog world "

It is here you learn actual practical learnings, experience, and exposure to the real competitive world !!

And I was very fortunate to enter this best college in one life at a very young age of 22 ..... with a lot of training, exposure, and experience which I got with my 3 years of my married life & 2 years of my motherhood experience !!

Also, I learned a lot through my failures & mistakes which were the stepping stone to whatever little success I could achieve in my life !!

Also, I would say I am still learning & having value addition in myself by regularly attending business seminars, short term management & entrepreneurship courses, exposing myself to a different way of working & this learning will go on till o die !!

I have to learn, unlearn & relearn !!

So I would like to say in today's world we should have the best education possible ..... But we would learn actual lessons of life by making mistakes & failing many times before we could achieve success !!

Family & husband support

It has been a mixed bag for me in terms of family support!! I never got much support from my in-laws
But was very fortunate that in Akash I have the world's most loving, caring, friendly but very strict hubby who is very passionate about his wife's success !!

He is my motivation, inspiration, and fear factor (because he is a very hard taskmaster and always after me whether it's my diet, my exercise, my social relationship & or everything else)

It is he who is very ambitious ... But not for himself but for me & he always says "Shilpa I will be very proud if I am known as Shilpa Agrawal's husband rather than Akash Agrawal "

He is my friend, philosopher, guide, coach, and guru. ..... He is my everything! Since he is always firmly behind me I don't need the support of anybody else !!

Success & failure

For me Success is not built on success it is built on failure ..... A person who avoids failure also avoids success! My short life history till now totally supports the above saying !!

We have the example of Abraham Lincoln ... Who lost all the elections he fought in his entire life before eventually winning the last but the biggest election in his life .... Presidential election of the USA !!

I believe it is only failures that give you humility, hunger, determination, and passion to achieve extraordinary success !!

Life philosophy

My philosophy in life is that people can guide you, motivate you .... but it is up to you who has to rise like Phoenix from ashes to be somebody in this world!

My inspiration

I have mentioned earlier that my hubby Akash is my greatest strength & he is the one who always tries to inspire me to achieve my true potential which he fills is at a world level !!

But I am also inspired by Indira Gandhi ...... I am inspired by the way she use to manage the country single-handedly, and the way she through her leadership fought several wars with Pakistan & won especially the Bangla liberation war !! Although I don't agree with her policies I admire & get inspired by her passion, determination, and courage to lead this very complex country single-handedly !!

Does life come to standstill for women after marriage & motherhood????

No, not at all ...... !! I would say it is the beginning of life for every woman!!

It is only marriage & motherhood which converts a girl (who is always protected, and restricted) into an all-powerful woman!!

It is only after marriage & motherhood a girl is metamorphosed into a woman who becomes the creator of the world by giving birth to a child, spreads love in the world by giving more love to her entire family than she gets in return, and spreads.... empathy, patience, multitasking ability in the world by managing family, children, personal & professional life !!

So I believe marriage & motherhood is the beginning of new life for every woman!!

My advice to all women

My dear most wonderful creation God has ever created In This universe ...... You all are born to excel ..... Born to spread love ...... Born to provide happiness, empathy, and friendship !!

Above are not just statements... I firmly believe In it!

I believe all women especially Indian / Asian women because of their upbringing & also because of there training/exposure they go through when they are married & during motherhood (through this journey they learn to manage their school as well as their home, their younger siblings, they are taught how to behave, they are taught empathy, multitasking, patience, etc) .... are born to excel in whatever they want to do !!

Also, I believe ..... If more and more women take lead in business, politics, and leadership .... There will be no intolerance in society ..... the world will be far more prosperous, liveable, peaceful, and happy place than what it is today !!

www.ingramcontent.com/pod-product-compliance
Lightning Source LLC
Chambersburg PA
CBHW061436160726
47995CB00003B/916